D1508412

Letters

Library of Congress Cataloging in Publication Data

Allington, Richard L.
  Letters.

  (Beginning to learn about)
  Summary: Introduces the letters A to Z through a
word guessing game and repeated examples of letters
matched with corresponding words.
  1. English language—Alphabet—Juvenile literature.
2. Word games—Juvenile literature. [1. Alphabet.
2. Word games. 3. Games] I. Krull, Kathleen.
II. Garcia, Tom, ill. III. Title. IV. Series.
PE1155.A48 1982   [E]   82-9785
ISBN 0-8172-1384-8   AACR2

Library of Congress Number: 82-9785

  2 3 4 5 6 7 8 9 0 86 85 84

Printed in the United States of America.

Richard L. Allington is Associate Professor, Department of Reading,
State University of New York at Albany.
Kathleen Krull is the author of twenty-nine books for children.

BEGINNING TO LEARN ABOUT

LETTERS

BY RICHARD L. ALLINGTON, PH.D., · AND KATHLEEN KRULL

ILLUSTRATED BY TOM GARCIA

Raintree Childrens Books · Milwaukee · Toronto · Mexico City · London

With your finger, trace the letters.
Follow the arrows.

Say the names of these animals.
Say the letters that begin their names.

Turn the page for the answer.

F f fish

L l lion

Say the names of these animals.
Say the letters that begin their names.

Then turn the page.

K k kangaroo

B b butterfly

Say the names. Say the letters.

P p pig

ant **A a**

Say the words. Say the letters.

cat **C c**

X x

X ray

Say the words. Say the letters.

J j jump rope

spider **S s**

Say the words. Say the letters.

E e elephant

violin V v

Say the words. Say the letters.

Q q
queen

H h
horse

Say the words. Say the letters.

newspaper

Nn

Uu unicorn

Say the words. Say the letters.

D d dragon

ice cream I i

Say the words. Say the letters.

M m

monkey

yo-yo

Y y

Say the words. Say the letters.

W w walrus

octopus # O o

Say the words. Say the letters.

Z z zebra

rainbow **R r**

Say the words. Say the letters.

T t tiger

grasshopper **G g**

Now look carefully. Can you find
the letters of the alphabet?

Say them out loud.

Make your own alphabet book.
Look at a newspaper or magazine.
Find pictures of things that begin
with the letters **A** to **Z**.
Find letters to match each picture.
Cut out the pictures and the letters.
Tape or paste them onto pieces of paper.
Put the pieces of paper together in the order
of the alphabet.
Fasten them together. You may ask an adult to help you.

Look at this sentence:

A quick brown fox jumped over the lazy dogs.

Can you find all the letters of the alphabet in this sentence?
Write your own sentence (or ask someone to help you).
Try to use as many letters of the alphabet as you can.